Lean management for families

1. Edition May 2020

Bibliographic information from the German National Library: the German National Library lists this publication in the German National Bibliography; detailed bibliographical data can be found on the Internet at http://dnb.dnb.de

© 2020 Frau Ordnung

Producer and Publisher: BoD – Books on Demand, Norderstedt

ISBN: 978-3-7519-5804-2

Lean management for families

Less stress, more time, without sacrifice

Frau Ordnung

To Kelvin und Kira.

Thank you!

Contents

My vision 13

Invitation 15

How this book got produced 19

About this book 27

The methods 31

General note about Lean 33

The value of streams 33

KANBAN: Visualisation of family plans 34

KAIZEN: Continuous Improvement Process CIP 37

MUDA: The 7 forms of waste 40

5S: clearing out sustainably 46

HANSEI: Reflection with Maslow 53

Other methods 58

JIT "Just In Time" – the 5R's 58

Jidoka – intelligent automation 60

Pull-Principle 61

Summary 65

The implementation 67

Before you get started 69

The entrance area 70

Kitchen 71

Living room 75

I

Bathroom / Toilet 77

Bedroom 80

Children's room 84

Guest room...87

Home-Office / Workspace 88

Basement..90

Hobby room / musician's room / gym / crafts / garage 92

Garden..96

Summary **99**

The most important principles in a nutshell 102

One year living LEAN **105**

The big picture 107

1st month   -   HANSEI................................108

2nd month   -   5S...110

3rd month   -   KANBAN..............................112

4th month   -   Streams 113

5th month   -   KAIZEN 116

6th month   -   Success 118

7th month   -   HANSEI II.............................118

8th month   -   5S II......................................119

9th month   -   Streams II 120

10th month   -   KAIZEN II 121

11th month   -   MUDA................................122

12th month   -   Success 123

Prospect..125

II

Motivating quotes 127

Literature 133

Thank you 137

About the author 141

INDEX 145

My vision

Living with children is precious. A family is valuable. But also exhausting. In the past, but especially nowadays, parents are under enormous pressure to expect. From the inside as from the outside.

However, when parents use lean management at home, they achieve exactly the same results that are achieved in the large manufacturing companies:

more time, less costs and even less stress.

The implementation of the lean principles is so simple and trivial, and yet hardly any father or mother knows them. The basics are not taught at school and by parents. Some parents have heard of lean management for work reasons but did not come up with the idea of applying these principles in the household.

I want to help these parents!

I want to take the burden of tearing them apart. Not being able to withstand the pressure anymore. I want to show the mothers that they have the strength and above all the skills to live in a stress-free family, to be able to save money and finally have more time for themselves. I want to show the fathers that lean management in the household is not rocket science but offers extreme support to women.

To be able to remember the things that are important to you and to be able to let go of things that do not make you happy - that is my goal!

Invitation

I would like to invite you to connect with me - you can find me personally on the popular social channels Facebook, Instagram and Twitter.

You can also join the Facebook community "#LeanLiving" - in this group you will find like-minded people who support and enrich each other with tips and tricks from everyday life.

From time to time I give further information there and would like to make open networking possible.

You can find more detailed information on the 5S method mentioned in this book in my book "Lean in the household - mucking out sustainably with 5S".

The addresses for the individual profiles:

Facebook:	www.facebook.com/frauordnung0711
Instagram:	www.instagram.com/frauordnung0711
Twitter:	twitter.com/Frau_Ordnung
Facebook-Group:	www.facebook.com/groups/leanlivingnow
Website:	www.frauordnung.de

If you always do what you always did,
you'll always get what you've always got.

Henry Ford

How this book got produced

February 1979. One of the toughest winters of weather records in Germany. I was born in February as the oldest of four children, in completely snow-covered northern Germany. My parents didn't even know at the time whether they would make it all the way back from southern Germany, where my father's parents lived, to the north. Four years later, for the first time in my life, I learned what "lean" means - but without being able to call it by name: we moved. From the north to the south.

My first childhood memory: how I had to leave behind my beloved "duck", a yellow 2CV that my father gave me for my 3rd birthday after he disassembled it to sell the expensive pieces. My parents didn't have much money and so everything we wanted to take with us had to fit on a trailer without a tarp. I was allowed to take my rocking horse and my favourite teddy bear with me. The trailer was packed to the smallest centimetre, avoiding wasted space was absolutely necessary here.

It was only a few days before the duck was forgotten.

What I learned from that episode: good planning is essential, waste of space is to be avoided and every now and then you just have to sort things out in life. It can hurt for a while, but it doesn't have to.

I still have a photo of the duck in my photo album, which I cherish.

Daughter and big sister

Over the next few years, I learned one thing above all: a household with four children requires a lot of organization, delegation and tolerance. All family members must also abide by rules, otherwise chaos will break out at some point.

In my parents' house, I learned a lot about avoiding waste because everything was kept, repaired, reused and saved. My mother made meal plans every week so that she exactly knew what to buy on her weekly bulk buying in such a way that, firstly, the household money was sufficient and secondly, no food had to be thrown away.

The household chores were also split up and adjusted for each child according to their abilities (we were all born 4 years apart). Cleanliness and order, a lean catchphrase that we will encounter again with the 5S, often came first. Sweeping, vacuuming, cleaning the bathroom, laying the table, operating the dishwasher, ironing, mowing the lawn - which is just what happens in an ordinary household.

When I was 12, I was introduced to the great art of ironing men's shirts - in such a way that the shirt was ironed perfectly in the shortest possible time. If you have ironed the laundry mountain of a family of six for several years, you know that any unnecessary movement, reworking and ironing is a waste of time.

With a large amount of knowledge in housekeeping and manual work (I could still build a concrete wall today), my parents released me to Stuttgart at the age of 19 to study at the University of Applied Sciences for library and information technology.

University

A small 12 square meter student dormitory was waiting for me. Not a lot of space for all the things you had accumulated in your childhood and youth. But I had the fixed idea that I really wanted to put everything that was mine in this room. And so I looked for and collected every thing, every book, every single memento from my parents' house and stuffed it into my own little room. I had never had an own room before and just wanted to know what really belongs to me alone. With three siblings you are used to sharing everything.

Back then I became painfully aware of the problem of having "too much of everything". Determined not to want to live in a lumber room for the next three years, I automatically applied the first "S" of the 5S lean tool: I sorted out. After that I put the remaining things properly, cleaned the whole room until it flashed and was happy about my new, fresh and tidy home.

I also mastered my studies with lean criteria: the time you have as a young person does not want to be wasted. Right from the start I set up a structured plan, which courses had to be completed when and where and with what result. I did not attend courses that were not useful. Since I was - by the way - one of the laziest students of the whole semester, this was REALLY necessary. Because if you want to receive your diploma in the given time, you need to know exactly what the goal is and what is leading you there. Wasted time is out of place here.

Mother

A few years later I got a new role in which I was able to apply my entire lean knowledge again: in 2009 and 2012 my children were born. The father: a successful management consultant specialized in lean management.

For the first time in my life, some ways of life suddenly got names. I heard about "5S" and the "Continuous Improvement Process", read books about "Value Stream Oriented Process Management" and "The 7 Forms of Waste". I had intuitively implemented a lot of lean things, now I realized why some behaviours were good for me. I finally understood that my constant questioning "Why?" in lean management is a successful questioning technique, extremely purposeful and effective.

Life as a family manager in a lean-led household is relatively stress-free and pleasant. However, I often admired friends who turned out to be true improvisation artists because again something was not planned right to the end, the children were missing some things and they remained so calm. And I assumed that everyone just made more money than I did because they apparently had the budget to buy some things double and triple.

... and my personal crisis

One day, as a successful family manager, I had to admit that living in a golden cage was not my goal in life. I had everything you could ask for except a man who was there for his family. Often alone at home, not random from Sunday evening to Thursday night. Plus two small children. No childcare options, but also no pressure to go to work.

During this time, I was heavily involved in volunteer work, managed children's crawling groups, helped other mothers who were in need of care, sewed nice things for a small online shop, took care of our private renovation - shortly after the birth of our son we bought an brand new "old" apartment that needed to be renovated - and tried to be as efficient as possible to find half an hour for myself at the end of the day.

Which just got too much at some point.

This episode was followed by a short and painless moving out of the shared apartment and one year later the successful introduction of the switching model for the children. Since then, our children are changing apartments every Sunday evening for one week.

And it works.

And the lean principles also helped me from the start. Focus on the goal, avoid potential waste types, clear communication, standardize many processes and above all work on continuous improvement. The children are getting older, situations are changing and thanks to Lean, this hurdle has also been overcome.

It has been the biggest crisis I had faced so far.

Corona

And then it was Friday, March 13th, 2020. The COVID-19-lockdown in southern Germany. Right in the middle of my weekly business network, we get the message: schools will be closed till the end of the Easter holidays. Three long weeks of home schooling, two weeks of Easter vacation. And with a little note: maybe.

A virus almost is bringing the world to a standstill. Millions of people are sent to their home offices and are no longer allowed to go to work. From now on, pupils and students have to learn at home immediately and receive new school assignments from the teachers every day. Couples who normally only see each other in the evening now have to get along with each other every day, share their home office and living room table, and at the same time discuss who cares for the children.

In such crises, lean management at home really proves its worth.

Stock purchases? We don't need it. We buy everything once a week, exactly the quantities that are needed. Thanks to the weekly meal plan, we know exactly what we need. Food is not wasted, nor is the space in the kitchen.

Home Schooling? The children created their own timetables. With breaks, favourite subjects, less-loved subjects, long and short school days and everything that goes with it. The numerous e-mails with school assignments are printed out immediately, sorted for the children and dealt with accordingly the next day.

My husband and I - shortly after the first crisis I was lucky enough to meet this wonderfully chaotic person - share childcare with us. He in the morning, me in the afternoon. If the children do schoolwork in the morning, he can work on the side. When I do my part in the afternoon, we prefer sports and music lessons when we can go outside and don't disturb him. We can go into the forest, soak up the sun, strengthen the immune system and practice drums and piano.

In the evening, we adults can consider whether we want to work on something that has been left behind or enjoy the end of the day.

The lean methods of standardization and constant process improvement support us here every day.

Changes in the job

Since I work as a professional organizer for my customers at their homes, this crisis also hit me hard professionally. I was no longer allowed to go to my customers, give lectures or give courses. I was about to put my head in the sand and wonder if I could still maintain this business model. And as so often in life, when I am faced with a difficult situation, I asked myself: Which lean principle can help me now? There must be something!

And yes - I focused on reflection and visualization. HANSEI and KANBAN are the Japanese terms for both tools. Was it a mistake to only serve "offline" customers? Can't I go online? What do I have to do to achieve this goal, what are the possibilities for improvement?

And there it was again - the flow. The flow that lean consultants like to talk about when "everything is flowing", when the entire process chain is perfect and when it is fun to get closer to your goal at any point.

The result was overwhelming: after one week I was able to launch my online business, I designed concepts for webinars and online courses. I published a first book "Lean in the household: mucking out sustainably with 5S". I successfully encouraged the adult education centres to offer my courses as digital courses over the next two months. And was able to minimize the loss of earnings a little each time.

Today you have another result in your hands:

LEAN MANAGEMENT FOR FAMILIES.

Your family may be different from mine. Your life for sure. But your family has dreams, goals, and needs as well. And your life also goes through many different phases.

Lean management for families can bring support to every family in every phase of life. Whether you have three children who are in school or university. Whether your first baby was just born. Even as a new grandparent, *Lean management for families* can help you meet the individual needs, goals, and desires of each family member!

The lean concept can be used regardless of life situation or family status, which is what makes this method so incredibly valuable and successful!

1

About this book

Settle one difficulty,
and you keep a hundred away.

Confucius

I would like to encourage you to use lean in your family, to familiarize yourself with the methods and tools and to gain more freedom and more time for yourself step by step, for everyone in your family. I wish you and your family members to recognize what your real-life goals are, what you want for your life and achieve this!

You bought this book because you want to change something in your life. And you will! With LEAN MANAGEMENT FOR FAMILIES it is possible to relieve stress, to find time that was long lost and to be clear about what your personal priorities are and what you can detach yourself from in the future.

In this book you will learn a lot about the individual lean tools, but you will also receive numerous practical tips.

I recommend that you first work through the chapters in the first part of the book on the individual methods. In the second part of the book, you can choose which chapter to start with. Here you will find practical tips and hints for the usual rooms in a household.

Grab a pen!

I got used to reading books with a pencil in my hand and many of these little colourful sticky notes to stick on. Take a pen and mark the passages that are important to you! Scribble on the edge, take notes - this book is meant to help you work on your situation, change the situation. Take this opportunity and see this book as your most important tool on the way to a happier and more organized life.

And now I wish you a good start and lots of fun reading, labelling and above all: when implementing!

2

The methods

I hear and I forget.
I see and I remember.
I do and I understand.

Confucius

General note about Lean

The basic principle of lean thinking is quite simple: at its core it is about avoiding waste of any kind. Both in the processes and in the materials used.

In this way, all activities that are necessary to achieve the goal should be optimally coordinated.

If you apply lean management consistently, you can expect 30% more time and 30% less costs in the first year - that is the minimum. Do the math: with Lean in the family, you can save almost seven hours on a 24-hour day! And who would not like to have 30% more salary - without a promotion ...

But now to the individual principles and methods:

The value of streams

In family life, this means first of all questioning what the real goals of each individual are. This is not just about the big goals in life, but also about the small goals. Some want to experience a sporting event, run a marathon - others want to achieve success in business life. Children want to graduate from school or successfully complete an apprenticeship.

Everyone may want to develop personally, meet friends and family, expand their social environment and enjoy.

The partnership should be a harmonious coexistence and not a stressed relationship that takes more strength than gives.

Environmentally conscious families want to do something good for nature, improve their own carbon footprint, experience a sustainably managed household.

Whatever goals you strive for - in the sense of lean management, you may achieve them in the most effective way without indirections. Obstacles are overcome and used as opportunities. You are in a constant process of further development and improvement.

There are various methods and tools with which lean management can be implemented in the family.

In the next chapters I will explain the differences between the individual methods that can be used in a family. You can decide whether, and if so, which ones.

In the second part of the book, the practical part, I will always refer to the individual methods so that the first part can be understood as a reference work and knowledge repository.

KANBAN: Visualisation of family plans

KANBAN means "sign" or "sign" in Japanese. In companies and productions, you will often find so-called KANBAN boards, large boards or walls on which processes, planning steps and other topics are depicted with numerous coloured symbols and markers.

With a KANBAN board in a family, you have the opportunity to get an overview of the individual activities and dates.

Another important aspect is that you no longer delegate (or have to) responsibility for planning the individual obligations, but the entire family is involved in the planning.

You also get an overview of the bottlenecks, the bottlenecks in your family.

The big overview

With the visualization of all your needs, actions and appointments, every family member knows what is actually going on in the lives of others.

In order not to lose the overview, the most important things are discussed every week during a 15-minute family appointment and the data is updated accordingly. Mostly Sunday evening is suitable.

Even large dates that affect society or life around the family can be noted here. Holidays, events, political events - whatever is important for family planning is brought together here and recorded visibly for everyone.

The meal plan for the coming week is also part of the KANBAN visualization. During your family appointment, discuss what wishes there are, what you want to cook and when, and who goes shopping the items and food that are needed.

Not only do you avoid waste because you have bought too much or unnecessary groceries, you also take away the stress of having to quickly think about what to cook for the family during the week when there is no time for planning whether the children like it.

Families living separated

A special feature here are separated parents, with whom the children live in an alternating model. As part of the KANBAN visualization, appointments are also recorded here that are important for the children, but take place during the time when they are with the other parent.

In this way, the children feel that it is important for both parents to participate in their lives. It also helps a lot for your own planning if you know which events or excursions are taking place or are planned. Misunderstandings and disappointments can be avoided if, for example, the big surprise visit to the amusement park is answered with "But we were there last week!".

Overnight stays or visits to friends can be announced and recorded in this way as well as birthday invitations or other events.

Implementing

Use a large whiteboard, a blackboard or simply a large pin board for the implementation. Attach this board in a central location, perhaps in the hallway or on the kitchen wall.

There should be a place for an annual calendar on this board, for example a detailed two-week plan, a meal plan and space for receipts that have to be processed. Open invoices, letters to be answered, birthday invitations.

And then plan a weekly recurring appointment for a family meeting.

That way, you will no longer experience surprising schedule collisions and the wishes and needs of each individual family member can be considered.

KAIZEN: Continuous Improvement Process CIP

KAIZEN or also known as CIP – the Continuous Improvement Process.

KAIZEN originally meant that problems should not be viewed as negative obstacles, but as positive challenges.

5 steps are used to solve problems and ensure improvements.

The 5 KAIZEN-Steps

Step 1

Describe the current situation, how things are behaving and why. This is part of the inventory, the so-called actual analysis.

Step 2

Think about how you would like the situation to be in the future. What would be the goal? Try to visualize your desired state in as much detail as possible and picture every detail in your mind's eye as precisely as possible.

Step 3

Decide on a new routine, a new habit that is easy for you to change and that you can implement easily and quickly. Make sure that the new routine really brings you closer to the target state.

Step 4

Start the next day, in any case in the same week, with the implementation of the new routine. Always make a note of suggestions for improvement in order to permanently improve the new habit. Correct if necessary and carry out fine adjustment.

Step 5

Stay tuned. Make sure that the new routine brings you closer to the desired goal from step 1 and that it is sustainable and long-lasting.

But how to start?

Always decide on one suggestion for improvement, on one process that you would like to change. Do not start the next one until you have completed the first improvement! Otherwise you run the risk of overexerting yourself and the frustration of countless unending changes wins out.

It is equally important that you begin the change in the next seven days. The idea of calling this period the very personal "KAIZEN week" is popular. This week, you concentrate entirely on reaching the desired target state from the problem.

Do not see the problems or shortcomings as problems, look optimistically at the new opportunities that arise!

Take before / after photos! Be sure to record step 1 in writing, document the current situation and all further steps. If your improvement has prevailed, you will often not be able to remember the beginning at the end.

As a Professional Organizer, I like to do before and after photos at the customer's site. If I then present the before pictures, most can hardly believe how it should have looked before.

The most important final step is then to monitor the changes. Be sensitive to whether the changes lead to the desired result or need to be adjusted further. Make notes and write down the things that you actually wanted to toast but did not make it in the first week so that they are not forgotten.

KAIZEN is a lifestile

The other name, the "continuous improvement process" clearly suggests that KAIZEN is like a philosophy of life. However, this is not a modified form of "higher, faster, further" - it is about always questioning, solving and then improving the current problems.

It is even more important that you celebrate the improvements! Celebrate the newfound freedom to feel that you've finally solved the core problem! Enjoy the moment and be completely in the present.

Continuous improvement does not mean continuous work - it means continually celebrating the achievements.

MUDA: The 7 forms of waste

The seven forms of waste accompany us as a lifelong process. On the way to achieving our goals as a family, but also as independent people, we always encounter one or the other type of waste. If you come across a problem and are not sure whether it is a process problem or a type of waste, you can stick to the basic thesis:

All activities and processes that cause costs or suffering but do not create value or do not bring you closer to your goal are wasted.

There are seven different forms of waste:

1. Overproduction

If you've cooked more than the whole family can eat. When the fish in your aquarium have more babies you can keep so you have to buy a larger one.

In family life, this can also be seen in today's consumer behavior: what do you consume or use too much? Too much fast food, too much sweets, too much alcohol, too much streaming television, too much smartphone use ...

Overproduction always occurs when you have created or done more than you should have done.

One solution that can be used to identify overproduction very well is the value stream analysis already mentioned.

2. Inventory

It's the mountain of things in a family household. Collecting and hoarding items clearly belongs in this category of waste.

That form of waste always arises when you have bought more than you actually need. Bulk packs of food that expired before you could eat them. Also storing objects and things that you don't actually want in your household anymore.

Because of their own small cellar, some families rent an external storage room in order to store the stocks there.

Stocks can be resolved very well using the 5S method. You can read a brief summary of exactly how this method works in the following chapter or in the book "Lean in the household - mucking out sustainably with 5S", in which I go into detail about this individual tool.

3. Correction and defects

This type of waste usually arises when you want to complete a task quickly and later realize that you have to do it again.

If a part of the backrest has broken off on the wooden chair and you glue this part in place, as this is the fastest way. Unfortunately, the piece breaks off a short time later because the glue - which you already knew when gluing - is not up to the load. So now you have to get the tool and screw the back together and dowel. The time you used to glue was wasted.

You may also have found yourself that you only briefly scanned an important email in the morning. In the evening you find that in the morning you forgot to write down the appointment that was mentioned in the email. So you have to turn on the computer again, search for the email and open it, to finally note the appointment.

4. Waiting

How often do we have to wait for other people within the family? Is it possible to change this with a timetable or schedule?

Check whether the appointments of the individual family members are coordinated. Plan for buffer times, but do not calculate too freely.

We often fail because we do not communicate the dates clearly and misunderstandings arise.

When your partner announces "likely to be home for dinner" - does he really know when you planned to have dinner prepared? And what do you do if he didn't make it to dinner?

Both are involved here: You have to communicate very clearly: "Dinner will be ready at 6 pm; since I cook something this evening, it may be cold afterwards." Your partner must also communicate if he gets a business appointment in between during the day: "Honey, I can't make it until 6 pm today - don't wait for me.". Or also: "There was an unscheduled appointment - is it possible that we can eat half an hour later?"

With this clear communication you avoid unnecessary waiting times, which lead to dissatisfaction on both sides.

5. Unnecessary Transport

When we drive things back and forth without coordinating them beforehand. Driving the child to school in the morning because you planned to pick them up on the way home in the afternoon. At lunchtime you remember that you urgently need something else from home for the project in the company - you had forgotten the documents at home. So you drive the same route again. Until you remember that your son wanted to go home with a friend today - and in the morning you drove the car for free. The child usually ends up taking the bus to school.

If you have already moved, you also know what unnecessary transportation means. You may have unnecessarily carried more than one box from one room to the next after unpacking the box, only to discover a few days later that the box was not correctly labeled and you would carry it back to the room from which you were carrying it just in the beginning.

You can avoid unnecessary transport routes through good planning - when must who be where with which activities? Do you have the option of using public transport instead of having to make unnecessary detours in the rush hour in the city traffic in order to arrive at your appointment on time?

6. Unnecessary Movement

This primarily includes searching for things. How much time do you spend walking around the house looking for things?

Make a list of the ten things you are most looking for and determine a place where they will be kept in the future. And then once and for all.

Also closely tied to the unnecessary movements above – is one type of waste "empty walks". If you live in a multi-story house, you can get used to take something with you every time that has to change floors, whether on the way from bottom to top or vice versa. This way you avoid running the one route empty-handed, only to have to cover the distance again to get the things you need.

7. Overprocessing

Overworking or overfulfilling behaves similarly to overproduction. Processes can also be viewed here:

You still don't know if you will get your vacation approved in August - but you plan your vacation in case it gets approved. It took three evenings full of anticipation. When your vacation application is rejected, you are disappointed and upset about the time you have already spent planning.

You avoid overwork by always questioning whether the thoughts you are currently thinking are really effective. You may refrain from purely speculative thoughts in which you may be disappointed if you fail to do so. This also includes typical unnecessary worries. The more you worry, that is, you "overwork the brain" with theses and speculations, the more dissatisfied you become in your basic attitude to life. You are welcome to have a lot of thoughts - if you bring them closer to your actual goals. Overworking or overfulfilling are more thoughts than necessary, which often do not help you.

HADOME – the „5 Whys"

When searching for the individual types of waste, the questioning technique HADOME generally helps you. In this way, you get to the bottom of the actual core and not only fight the symptoms in an overambitious way.

One example - food waste

You spend too much money on food every month.

Why? Because you throw away more than you can process and eat. Why? Because when the food is on the table you are already fed up with snacks. Why? Because you usually only shop in a hectic and spontaneous manner when the family is already hungry. Why? Because you don't plan in advance what you want to cook during the week. Why? Because you hadn't taken the time to do it on Sunday evening.

And with that, you have found the real essence of the problem - if you were to think about a weekly schedule on Sunday evening, you could schedule weekly shopping on Monday and would have already done the shopping for the whole week in advance. In this case, you can even plan for any leftovers and pack them in the lunch boxes for work or school the next day if anything is left.

It is only important with this question that you ask "why" exactly 5 times - with two or three "why" you usually do not reach the actual problem, with too many "why" you are at some point in a discussion about God and the world and wondering what the meaning of life is ...

5S: clearing out sustainably

Who does not know that? In every corner there are undefined piles of paper, odds and ends, and things that haven't been put back to the places they belong.

As already mentioned with the 7 forms of waste, stocks accumulate in many households. Things that we were given at some point, bought too much, or simply did their job and have since ceased to exist in any corner of the house.

With the 5S method, everyone can maintain order in a sustainable and permanent manner at any location.

5 steps show a clearly structured procedure to throw off ballast and fill his house with the things that make your heart beat.

Why live in a household full of unpleasant possessions when you can feel comfortable and only surround yourself with the things that really give you pleasure?

The greatest advantages of order in the household

Whoever allows order in his household saves three very important things: time, money and nerves.

How often do you look for things? Car keys, glasses, any work or school documents. We are always searching for misplaced things that we have forgotten where we actually put them. A not insignificant part of our lifetime is wasted looking for things.

Annoyed, one often gives up the search to buy the desired item in the nearest shop. Sometimes, even without a previous search, you are pretty sure that you no longer have this article in your household. What a surprise if weeks or months later this part appears again! And at that moment you realize that you could have saved the money.

You can also save yourself the stress that you experience during the search and retrieval of the supposedly lost item.

With the 5S method you get an extremely powerful tool that is simple, so simple and explainable that even the smallest children can understand and implement it.

I dedicated a book to this topic: "Lean in the household - mucking out sustainably with 5S". If you want to take a closer look at the method presented here, you will find detailed descriptions and practical instructions with numerous examples.

The fact is: With the 5S method you can create order in the smallest corners of the household, but you can also limit yourself to a small part at the beginning.

Whether you choose the one drawer in your wardrobe, whether it should be the whole wardrobe or possibly the whole bedroom. It is up to you where you start with the 5 steps!

And little by little you can muck out the entire household with these 5 simple steps and keep it tidy. We all want this beautiful, liberated state to last as long as possible!

And this is also a characteristic of the true lean thought. It is about durability and the big picture, not about overzealous one-off actions created in stressed-out actionism.

The 5 steps in detail

#1: SEIRI: Sorting out

It all starts with sorting out the unneeded and unloved things.

Whatever place, wherever you have chosen and made it: you take all the things that are there and put them on the table, on the floor, on the bed. Wherever you want to start. Clear the place where you want to create order completely empty.

And then you take each of the parts individually and ask yourself the key question: "Does this thing make me happy?". Does this object fill you with joy? Does your heart open up when you look at it or use it?

Especially with everyday objects, this question sometimes appears a bit esoteric, but here it has its full raison d'être, too.

Whether for envelopes, screwdrivers or dresses: you know exactly whether there are some envelopes for which the adhesive rubber has long ceased to work; which screwdriver you generally take in hand when there is something to adjust; in which dress you feel comfortable and in which not.

If you are armed with this key question, you will save yourself all discussions about inherited and gifted things in your household. The price also does not matter if the item does not satisfy you one hundred percent!

Usually 50 - 80 percent of all items are sorted out and then sold, donated, given away or actually taken to the recycling center.

You don't have to keep old boards in the basement that belong to cupboards that you no longer have. You know that and I know that. The pain of putting these boards on the bulky waste will be limited.

Children will also be happy to sort out the question of whether this or that toy really makes them happy. It is usually the parents who are horrified because children do not care whether the expensive model ship was once a gift from grandma or the educational board game that Santa put under the Christmas tree was actually incredibly expensive. Children point out very directly to "Mum, I really don't play with that."

#2: SEITON: Set in order

After sorting out, put back the things you really want to keep.

True to the motto "Every piece has its place", you decide where to keep which thing.

Take your time thinking about where the right place for each of these things is. Question whether the previous place was actually the right one or whether there might be a better one.

You can also ask children here. "Where does this thing live?" Where do the dolls live? Where does the action figure live? Where do the books live?

EXKURS: First in First Out - FIFO

Quite simply this means that the things that you put in the cupboard first are also removed first.

This method is particularly useful for food, i.e. in the pantry and in the refrigerator. If you put the new groceries in the cupboards after a purchase, make sure to take out the existing groceries, put the new ones in the back of the cupboard and put the old ones in front of the new goods when you put them back.

Take a look at this technique in the usual supermarkets: here you will always find the freshest goods with the longest expiration date on the back of the shelf.

By using the First In - First Out rule, you prevent food from running out and thus contribute to the more sustainable and environmentally friendly use of valuable raw materials and resources.

#3: SEISO: Shine

At the same time as step 2, check whether the items are clean and well-kept. The fallen button is sewn on before the coat is hung back in the closet. The kitchen appliances are thoroughly cleaned and serviced once. Coffee machines are descaled, washing machines thoroughly cleaned.

All the activities that you have pushed ahead of you are now being tackled. Things are repaired, equipment cleaned and furniture polished to a high gloss.

As the year progresses, there are additional checklists or plans that you can use to record the basic types of cleaning in the household. Clean windows, scrub balcony or terrace. Clear out the kitchen cupboards and clean. Make a cleaning plan and note these dates on your KANBAN board!

#4: SEIKETSU: Standardize

Never cleaning up again! To be too good to be true? No!

Because with this fourth step you lay the basics for a sustainable order in your household.

Create and think about standards and routines.

In the first place there are uniform labels and markings. Routine processes are just as important. Here you come back into contact with the value streams and the core idea of lean management - avoiding waste and unnecessary processes.

You defined a place for each thing in the previous step - now it is a matter of introducing the routine that everything you have removed from its assigned place will also be put back there.

How often do you have stress because it looks messy in the hallway? Because children, men and dogs simply thrown their school bags, work clothes and toys into a heap without coordination. The coats were quickly thrown onto the back of the sofa because there was no space on the coat hook in front of the door.

Establish rules and procedures together as a family. Whoever comes home puts his shoes in the shoe cabinet, the bag in the place assigned to it, the jacket on the hook. Most of the time, family members do not follow these routines if they are not practical or the place is occupied by other things that have definitely not to be placed there.

Check your previous processes - use your personal value stream analyzes from the first section of this chapter and set standards.

"Shadow boards" are often used in workshops. Large boards on the wall, on which you can see the outlines for the tools. If a tool is taken off the wall, you immediately know where it belongs when you put it back.

Uniform labeling of boxes, cartons and containers is also a method to set standards and clearly define which thing has its place in which place.

The effect of standards is, in fact, that you hardly have to tidy up, or even less after family members, because everything has its place and it is always tidy!

Sounds like a dream?

There is always a catch ... the last S in this row:

#5: SHITSUKE: Sustain / Self-discipline

It just doesn't work without self-discipline.

Anyone who got rid of his overwhelming collection of 75 promotional pens in the course of a removal campaign and then travels across the country again to collect promotional pens cannot help the first four steps either. Then it becomes difficult.

Also, in families: if no one adheres to all routines or processes and constantly refuses to do so, the family structure starts to falter.

Here it is important that everyone sticks together and everyone knows what is important to the other and why.

Just be aware of this fact. In most cases, the knowledge of this point is simply sufficient. Because as the saying goes: "Self-knowledge is the first way to get better."

The same rule applies here: celebrate your success! Reward yourself when a process works particularly well! However, in the case of mucking out, the reward quickly sets itself up: less cleaning, less tidying up, no more searching.

HANSEI: Reflection with Maslow

The lean concept lives from constant reflection and the desire to simply do things better than before.

To do this, you need to be aware of which goals and needs you actually want to have achieved in the future, whether these needs and goals have already been met in the present and what steps and measures you have taken in the past to achieve these goals.

The American psychologist Abraham Maslow created the Maslow hierarchy of needs, also known as the pyramid of needs, to make it clear which needs are actually important for each individual.

Maslow's hierarchy of needs

1. **Physiological needs** are basic needs such as eating, drinking, sleeping, clean air, warmth. If these basic needs are not met, our body and our thinking change to survival mode. Our first goal in life is to meet these basic needs.

2. **Safety needs** are a desire for a stable environment. War, divorce, job loss, death of a close person. These issues often leave our lives out of joint.

3. **Belongingness and love needs** – friendships, love, care. We have a great need for acceptance, we want to be loved and feel that we are understood and accepted as the person we are.

These three basic needs must be met so that the last two can be achieved at all. As deficit needs, they only cover deficiencies, while the next two needs are designed for the growth of each individual, i.e. growth needs. Anyone who suffers a deficiency in the first three categories of needs cannot grow in the last two categories.

The fourth need can either be counted among the deficit needs or treated as a growth need.

4. **Esteem needs** are self-related desires such as the desire for recognition and appreciation. This also includes the need to recognize yourself, to have a healthy self-confidence and to experience respect and recognition from others.

5. According to Maslow, the desire for **self-actualization** awakens at the latest when the first four needs can be met. Here, in a clear desire for growth, people can realize themselves and achieve their true goals. According to Maslow, this need will never be 100% satisfied and even the people who have reached this level are generally estimated at around 2%.

A person as an individual can only fulfill the next level of needs if there are no deficiency symptoms in the needs of the lower levels. We cannot realize ourselves if we do not feel accepted by our fellow human beings. If we cannot meet the basic needs for food, sleep and a comfortable home, even giving and taking love becomes difficult for family members.

Needs in a family

It is important that everyone in the family knows about each other and their own needs. Who has what goal in life, what do we want to achieve together as a family, but more importantly: what are the goals of each individual?

You may wish for a home of cheerfulness, with an exuberant mood, many visits from friends and relatives and a large family. For your partner it has always been the wish to consider his or her own house as a place of retreat, the haven of peace in turbulent life, in order to recharge and relax the own batteries.

Reflection

Take the time, preferably twice a year, to talk to your family about the individual needs. It's not about confrontation! The aim is to reflect together on what goal you are currently heading for and how you have progressed on the journey so far.

How many times have you written New Year's resolutions for yourself that you haven't achieved? Take the pressure off such customs and change your strategy.

You can sit down and reflect together twice a year, preferably at the turn of the year and in the middle of the year (when the summer holidays give you time anyway).

Take a large book and write down different categories: job / career, family life / friends, sporting goals, children, house / apartment - whatever. With a view to **the future**, write down the wishes and goals that come to mind.

Let your thoughts run free! What else do you want to achieve, what do you want to learn, in which area do you want to grow? The respective points can be assigned to individual family members or can also be shared goals. You may want to run a marathon, your partner is aiming to learn a new language, your daughter wants to graduate from high school, and it is important for the son to go to the concert of his favorite band.

It is important that you are relaxed, do not put yourself under pressure, but calmly philosophize, compile, and think. If your family does not talk about the basic needs of each individual family member, how should these wishes ever be fulfilled? And a fulfilled life is ultimately a wish of everyone.

Then talk about **the current situation** and whether everyone's basic needs have been met to such an extent that the goals and desires can be achieved at all. Where are you now? To do this, use Maslow's pyramid of needs.

Then deposit this book in a place that is accessible to all family members as a reference work. Everyone should have the opportunity to check and reflect for themselves again and again. Those who get the feeling of having lost the common thread for their lives due to the stress of everyday life can return to their actual goals and reorient themselves.

After half a year, get back together and have a look - what have you achieved in the past? What goals could be achieved? What else is there to do? Did something deteriorate and what worked well? Some wishes will have changed or been fulfilled. Did you learn that and did you grow where you intended?

Think about where to change the direction of travel, but above all remember: learn thinking *lean* instead of wasting!

Lean philosophy is about seeing mistakes and problems as opportunities and learning from them. There are always new opportunities and challenges and with the opportunity to reflect you can take advantage of these opportunities and shape the life of your family that you all want!

Other methods

In addition to the main methods of lean management, there are numerous tools that you can use to implement them. There are almost no limits, nor are there any constraints. With Lean everything can, but does not have to.

The following principles and tools can be used as food for thought, gladly when it comes to the purchase of new devices or when you question processes. Or just to philosophize about it and to discuss your own views. The two basic principles *Just In Time* and *Jidoka* in particular relate very strongly to manufacturing companies and less to household-related topics, which is why these - actually elementary principles - are only dealt with here in the last chapter.

JIT "Just In Time" – the 5R's

The just-in-time principle - or JIT for short - is one of the two pillars in the Toyota production system. In addition to the Jidoka principle, the basis of the entire world of lean ideas rests here.

Simple, and formulated for the purposes in this book, means that care should be taken to only deliver the products that are needed when the need is there.

In a household, this can mean that you only prepare food when you are hungry. That shopping is only done when the corresponding food has become empty.

In summary, the question about the 5R's is used here:

The right part, at the right time, in the right place, in the right quantity and in the right quality.

Let's imagine the following situation:

You are standing in the shower after a long day of work and have just brushed off. Suddenly the water stops flowing - there was a water pipe break on the street in front of the house and the water was turned off unexpectedly. What do you need first of all? The **right part** is undoubtedly a towel. And when do you need it, when is the **right time** for this towel? Now, pretty much immediately and on the spot. Where should the towel be, what is the **right place**? Ideally right next to the shower and not in the bedroom, at the other end of the hall. How many towels do you need, what is the **right amount**? A gentleman may be satisfied with a small towel - a lady with long hair is more likely to need two towels. And in what quality is the towel needed, what is the **right quality** here? It has to be clean, some would like a fluffy towel, the other doesn't care, the main thing is that it's dry.

The question of 5R's can help you analyze and review all of your household processes. When the 5R's consistently realize extremely efficient added value when looking at your processes and flows in the household and remove many obstacles.

In the example above, this would mean that the question of the best place for towels is: in the bathroom, in a closet next to the shower or bathtub. And not in the bedroom, in a chest of drawers next to the bed.

Jidoka – intelligent automation

Alongside JIT, this is the second pillar in the Toyota production system.

Thanks to Jidoka, errors in the processes can be recognized immediately and then rectified. It means that errors that occur during production are recognized immediately, the machine is then stopped and the mechanic is given the opportunity to immediately search for the error and rectify it. If this were not the case, the result would inevitably be high defective products, which would then be reworked or, in the worst case, have to be disposed of.

In the household there is a classic case of cooking or baking.

If I prepare a dish with spoiled food, I have to make sure that all the food is fresh and of the right quality while cooking. If I notice while cooking that something seems to be bad, I should not continue to cook and hope that I may have been wrong, only to have to throw away all of the food afterwards.

Likewise when washing laundry. Perhaps it has happened to you before: You have used too much detergent and the laundry has foamed hopelessly. In modern washing machines, a sensor detects that there is too much foam in the washing machine and aborts the washing program on the spot. You can then remove the laundry by hand or, alternatively, have the foam pumped out to continue the laundry. If the washing machine had not recognized the error, the laundry could have become unusable or the washing machine could have been damaged. So you can fix the problem and continue washing the laundry.

Pull-Principle

The pull principle is mostly used when Just In Time cannot be implemented for whatever reason. Let's take the kitchen area: You are planning to buy a new coffee machine.

If you knew exactly when you were drinking which coffee, at what time and which type you could use the just-in-time principle and ensure that this coffee was always exactly prepared by your machine at the desired time.

However, since most people drink their coffee sporadically, and certainly not at certain times, on weekends at other times than on weekdays, and possibly not at home for two weeks on vacation, the pull principle comes into play here.

So there is a choice of a french press with which you can quickly and cheaply prepare one liter of coffee from coffee powder. As another option, you could buy a fully automatic coffee machine that will give you numerous variations of freshly ground beans. And finally there is the coffee capsule machine, which also delivers all the coffee variations with pinpoint accuracy, but made from coffee pressed into capsules.

At this point, I do not want to consider the discussion about the environmentally harmful effects of single-use capsules or coffee that is not ecologically correct.

I assume that you already know that coffee is generally more harmful to the environment (based on your personal carbon footprint) than tea, for example, and we assume that it is also possible to use coffee capsules made from renewable raw materials, wood for example, with fairness to use traded coffee.

If you have a specific request, please write to me or do some research on the Internet - there are now numerous providers of alternative products.

Generally, this is what makes capsule machines so expensive. Such machines are best suited for occasional coffee drinkers who are willing to pay a higher price for the small amount of coffee they drink. After all, you want to enjoy this coffee to your heart's content! The question is whether it is worth buying a comparatively expensive coffee machine if you rarely drink coffee anyway.

Back to our core topic, the pull principle:

You can now compare the advantages and disadvantages of each coffee machine using a simple table:

Machine	Advantages	Disadvantages
French Press 1 L	- Cheapest acquisition costs - Little need for space - Quick preparation of large amounts of coffee - Low waste requirements	- Beans must already be ground (degree of freshness) - No selection of preparation types - No single portions - Second device for boiling water necessary
fully automatic coffee machine	- Large selection of preparation types - Single servings - Low waste requirements	- Expensive purchase costs - Big need of space - Mostly: large quantities of coffee beans (degree of freshness) - No large quantities can be prepared
Capsule machine	- Average acquisition costs - Large selection of preparation types - Single servings - Usually relatively small space requirement - Shortest preparation time	- High waste production - No large quantities can be prepared

Now it is important to know what type of coffee drinker you belong to. Do you like to drink larger amounts, for example a whole pot at the breakfast table? Do you prefer a method of preparation? Do you like to choose between different variations, with milk and without, with caffeine or decaffeinated? Do you often have guests for coffee and cake or do you usually drink a cup alone? How much time do you have and how big is your storage space? A final point can still be the topic of acquisition costs and running costs, but this is rather secondary.

You can now use the pull principle. This means that the goods are only made available when they are needed.

The combination of a very cheap French press and a capsule machine can make the most sense. For guests and larger quantities, the French press is the clear favorite - but if you are only a casual coffee drinker and then possibly also with different preparation methods, the capsule machine is an advantage. With a capsule machine, and also with the fully automatic coffee machine, the coffee is prepared exactly in the quantity and exactly at the time when you want to drink it.

If you use the French press, though you don't drink that much coffee you will produce too much coffee. If it has become cold or the taste is no longer satisfactory, you pour away the coffee that too much. If you enjoy hosting guests, but you only own a capsule machine you will most likely produce too much garbage.

The fully automatic coffee machine takes most of the time - if you do not have that and without time for intensive care, this variant is not useful.

Another short example is buying a big car. In order for you to be able to go on vacation and to store your luggage for the whole family, you need a large car. Question how often you experience a vacation in this dimension. And whether it makes more sense to rent the big car extra according to the pull principle, if there is a need. If you need the large amount of space 14 days a year and the remaining 50 weeks would be able to cope with a smaller car, it makes no sense to buy a large car.

Summary

Lean can therefore always be used when it comes to recurring processes or streams. You can think of a process as a long thread. Always pay attention to how your personal threads look. Is the process continuous and is it purposeful? Or is it more like a thread in which a large ball is cuddled in the middle, in between you don't really know where the thread is and many small to medium knots can be found on closer inspection. With Lean you can find the knots and balls, unravel the thread, smooth it and make it smooth and flowing again.

In the case of one-off processes, lean can even be harmful and should not necessarily be used.

A lean management consultant once explained the difference to me as follows:

"Imagine you decide to have a child. The process of childbirth may only happen once in your life. It was such an extraordinary and unique event that Lean would be absolutely harmful. Because then you would have to choose a short, timed and flawless Caesarean section birth, planned and, if possible, without obstacles. However, if you are the midwife who helps five children to be born every day, you can make this process lean from the midwife's perspective. You can prepare your materials accordingly, optimize the rooms in the delivery room and improve the stay of the expectant mothers so that they perceive the births as an absolutely positive event. Then Lean is the right choice. "

As always, it depends on the point of view.

Always remember that lean thinking thrives on thinking step by step. Do not fall into blind actionism and also pay attention to the methods and principles mentioned above that they fit your values, goals in life and wishes. You don't have to do everything you've read or learned.

Try it out, go piece by piece and above all:

Celebrate your successes!

In the following second part of the book I will now give you practical help and tips that are designed for the individual rooms in a house or apartment. You can start with the room that is most dear to your heart or just browse. Perhaps you will notice one or the other tip where you want to start your personal lean project!

3

The implementation

Just do it.

Nike

Before you get started

I like this quote from Bruce Lee: "Knowing is not enough, we must apply. Willing is not enough, we must do."

In most cases it's all about motivation to start.

You have to start somewhere. The main thing is that you do it!

Where exactly, in which room or at which point, with which process or what need you start depends solely on you.

Find your biggest problem and tackle it!

In the following chapters you will find practical tips for the implementation of the principles and methods from the first part of the book. Some situations may seem familiar to you, other situations may not exist in your family at all. A family, like every single family member, is an absolutely individual combination of different characters, with so many different desires and needs that no family is like the other.

The tips are therefore as general as possible, but you will certainly not see any need for one or the other tip or discover any benefit.

So try it out, test it, improve it and adapt the individual ideas for your household, your own family so that it suits you. Understand the next chapters as a store of ideas and browse whether you can discover something useful. I am sure that in every room you will find something that will help you on your way to more time, money and less stress!

So that you don't get lost in the house, the rooms are modeled on the classic single-family house. You may have fewer rooms in an apartment, but that all depends on your lifestyle and circumstances.

Do we want to start? Let's rock!

The entrance area

Usually there is a cloakroom and a shoe rack in the corridor or hallway.

When we enter our house or have invited guests, we want to give a pleasant first impression and feel good when we come home. Nobody likes to be slain by things as soon as they enter their realm or really want to clear the way into the actual living area.

Practical instructions

Start here with a generous 5S campaign and muck out all shoes and jackets that have become too small for children, that are broken or too worn. Next, check if you have somewhere in the house the opportunity to store the shoes you don't need as often. Winter boots in the basement, hiking shoes in the closet with the sports gear - try to put on just the few shoes in the entrance area that you need every day or every two to three days.

With jackets, be sure to hang only those you use every day.

A maximum of one small umbrella stand can still be found in the corner, a few decorative pictures on the wall or objects that you like belong in this area.

If you think of the 7 forms of waste and have the space for it, you can now deposit your shoe cleaning supplies here. This saves you time when you want to clean your shoes and you don't have to work through a cupboard with general cleaning agents in the kitchen before you even get a leather cloth and shoe polish.

In this way, you keep the process short and can immediately, just in time, if a pair of shoes needs cleaning, take a rag on the spot and get the job done.

Kitchen

The kitchen and the associated dining room are often the central space of a house. Here people cook, eat and live. Decisions are made and discussions are held when cooking together. In addition, most of the housework is done here - dishes have to be washed, purchases stowed, food prepared and the garbage collected.

So this room is perfect for our KANBAN board, the multi-planning tool for the whole family.

We ourselves have a somewhat older toy board that we found used on the thrift store. It can be opened and consists of a main part and two side wings. I painted the wooden frame white, the originally green blackboard color with black, because we personally liked that better. The outer panels are closed magnetically - we like to decorate them with a few selected sayings or funny postcards.

On the inside there are new unpaid invoices on the left, on the other inside there are invitation cards or tickets for future events.

In the middle is our 14-day weekly schedule, including birthdays and events, as well as a meal plan and household chores.

Practical instructions

Browse at flea markets or on the internet in online thrift stores for a wall board that is suitable for you. You will find countless different whiteboards, boards, pin boards in so many variations on the used goods market that there is something for every taste. It doesn't have to be foldable, a simple whiteboard is enough.

Then draw a table. In the top row, first write down "day of the week", then each family member receives a column and finally label the last three columns with "birthdays / events", "meals" and "household". Then draw 14 lines below and enter the days of the week for the next two weeks on the far left.

An example is outlined on the following page - the example deals with the KANBAN plan of a family of four and has space for individual appointments, birthdays or family-related events.

In addition, the meal plan is shown and household chores are distributed.

Please note that this plan is only intended to be a very rudimentary example for illustration and no attention has been paid to the design and layout.

Your personal KANBAN board may and should contain personal elements and decorations!

Weekday	Mum	Dad	Leon	Maria	Birthday / Events	Meals	Household
Monday	London					Ravioli	
Tuesday					Grandma (85)	Fish with vegetab.	
Wednesday		Paris	gift George	Carla visits		Burger	Paper waste
Thursday		Paris				pancakes	
Friday	HomeOffice					Fish sticks	
Saturday	Spa Claudia	Children	10 am departure!		Football match	barbecue	kitchen
Sunday		9pm flight 2 Berlin	2-6pm Bday Geor.		George (II)	Ratatouille	
Monday		Berlin				Potato gratin	
Tuesday			math exam			Spaghetti Tonno	
Wednesday	Yoga		Physics exam			Chicken Wings	windows
Thursday						Rice pudding	

Then plan when you want to organize your personal KANBAN appointment with the family! Sunday evening is best, the duration should be a maximum of 15 minutes. On this appointment, all family members sit together and announce possible changes to future appointments. Children like to stay with friends or have them visit, parents are sometimes away on business and not at home overnight.

You can also design the meal plan together - so there are no later undesirable discussions about unloved and thrown away food. You can then plan when and who will go shopping and schedule it so that you only have to shop once or twice during these weeks. So you have saved a lot of time again and avoid costs because you do not have to run aimlessly and in the hectic pace as usual.

As a further step, as in the hallway, you should muck out the kitchen using a 5S campaign. To do this, you put all the contents of all kitchen cabinets out of the kitchen - you can also use the worktops on the dining table, the floor, the sideboards, and of course you can also sort them.

Take each thing in your hand and sort out. Devices that you have not used for a long time and are used or that are broken can be sorted out. You also put the inherited porcelain and silverware, as well as vases, candle holders and other utensils to the test. When it comes to food, be careful about whether it has expired or can still be used, or whether you can process it in the near future before it is too late. Keep in mind which foods you buy too much of.

Then put things back, rethinking the basic order that was previously set up in the kitchen. Are all objects where it makes sense? Or do you have to run four different places in the kitchen to prepare a salad? Check the previous processes and whether they are optimally coordinated. Orient yourself on the basic rule "Every piece has its place".

Perhaps you also discussed at your KANBAN meeting that weekend cooking is done by the parent who has no time during the week? Grab a child and enjoy cooking as quality time together! In this way you have gained a lot of time for yourself and can also discover a new passion - trying out new recipes and foreign cooking cultures is worth a try. Some people have discovered their new passion here - and what used to be one of the stress factors in family life changes to one of the highlights of the week.

Living room

The living room is one of the main common areas. The wishes and needs of all family members meet here.

The 5S campaign is also suitable for the living room. Clear out everything that has no place in the living room and try to keep in mind that this room is used equally by all family members. A living room is neither an outsourced children's room nor a second home office.

Practical instructions

Now the HANSEI method is used: together with your partner, you can reflect on a quiet evening what the real desires of everyone are - if we are honest, it usually turns into several evenings.

Start with the **future** and ask yourself: where do you see yourself in one, in five, in ten years? What are your deep desires and needs? How did you imagine your future home as a child or teenager? Paint your future together in positive colors, imagine how your house should look in the future. Which needs should then be met and what must have changed in any case.

Then reflect on the **present**: where are you now? Which wishes are currently not being fulfilled or cannot be fulfilled? Are there reasons for this? How do you feel and what are your biggest construction sites within the family? Think of Maslow's pyramid of needs. Are the individual basic needs of all family members met?

Finally, you reflect on the **past**. What steps have you taken so far to achieve your future goals? What has been forgotten, what has been neglected? And what made you stand where you are today? What went well, what went less well?

As a couple, you should have found the common denominator here. If not, consider whether it might make sense at this point to talk to an uninvolved third party about it.

Lean also always means "lifelong learning". It is not about constantly optimizing and improving yourself and others. It's about seeing problems as opportunities for new things, being open to creative methods and possibilities and not giving up hope.

Repeat these HANSEI evenings once or twice a year. Shape your future actively and take your life into your own hands!

After all, the living room is also a retreat for cozy moments. Read books and magazines that will encourage and motivate you on your way. Biographies are very suitable - if you have a goal in mind and do not know how you want to achieve it: read biographies of people who have already achieved this goal!

At a primary school in the south of our town, I run past the following quote every day: "The head is round so that thinking can change direction." Be brave and use your head! They think! Whether loud and together, or quiet for yourself - the main thing is that you think.

Bathroom / Toilet

In the bathroom, many family needs often have to be met - mostly washing machine and dryer, bathing accessories, cosmetics, medicines, towels, dirty and clean laundry, toilet paper (a space-consuming utensil that should not be underestimated), decorative objects, sometimes also plants.

The methods and principles used here are the 5S method and checking the 7 forms of waste. The goal is to create space in the bathroom, save costs and give the room the special feel-good atmosphere that everyone can fully recharge their batteries here.

When we are on vacation and stay in a hotel, we are often happy about the clean and tidy bathroom. Almost spartan, there is a small bar of soap, a toothbrush jar and sometimes a few cosmetic samples up to the usual utensils such as cotton swabs and shower caps.

Why shouldn't our own bathroom be just as beautiful and offer us the added value of being able to relax, retreat and letting your soul dangle? How often do you go to your bathroom just to be able to leave it as quickly as possible? The main thing is to take a short shower and brush your teeth, but voluntarily relax in this chaos? No thanks!

Practical instructions

For the 5S campaign, remove all utensils from the bathroom, preferably in the kitchen. There you have a sufficiently large number of rubbish bins.

Expired products should in fact no longer be used. Expired drugs no longer anyway. Even old cosmetic products can have bacteria that no longer belong on your body. If you have a guilty conscience when disposing of it, you can reassure yourself that you will no longer have this problem in the future, that you have decided from now on to only buy what you really need.

This is where the fifth S comes into play - self-discipline is particularly important: do not buy bath products, shower gels, soaps, shampoos, nail polishes ... in stock. Especially with such products, large economy packs are not always worthwhile, since these have usually an expire date and the space in ordinary bathrooms is simply not there.

As a next step, check the 7 forms of waste: you can get a handle on bulk purchases, i.e. overproduction and warehousing, if you look closely.

Another big cost factor is hidden in the laundry area: how old is your current washing machine? Do you know how much energy you use per wash and do you also use the different programs? Modern washing machines often have eco washing programs, which may take significantly longer, but are very energy efficient. Invest in an ammeter that you switch between the socket and the washing machine. Such devices are usually available for cheap money in the hardware store. Get your current electricity price and calculate. Study the operating instructions for your washing machine and find out which washing cycles use less water and energy.

Sort your laundry correctly! In our household you will find four different stacks of laundry:

White / bright: wash with 60° C

Dark: wash with 60° C

White / bright: wash with 30° C

Dark: wash with 30° C

You can teach the children the basic rule when sorting laundry: everything that is worn directly on the body - underwear, socks, pajamas, bed linen - should be washed at 60° C. Everything else at 30° C.

For the 30° C washes, there is often a "quick mix" program in which you can only wash a small amount, but use the least water and energy. Use such programs for shirts or if you have laundry that needs to be washed, but which does not yet have enough "material" for a full wash load.

In the ecological sense, the question then arises whether a dryer should be purchased or not. On the one hand, it depends on the space. Some bathrooms have a very small floor space, but you can put the dryer on the washing machine. If you have the space for both devices, I can only advise you to buy a dryer.

Investing in an expensive device is really worthwhile here, because it actually saves a lot of time. The high price also makes sense for energy-saving reasons, because the inexpensive devices usually have a very high energy consumption, which in turn is responsible for the bad reputation of the dryer.

Nevertheless, with a good dryer you save time, money and effort. Since we started using a dryer, the mountain of ironing has decreased by 85%. The only items of clothing to be ironed are now shirts, a few pants made of special materials, and the tea towels and cloth napkins. The rest of the clothing can be folded up immediately and stowed in the closets. The energy that you use for the dryer can be saved without problems by not ironing. You can also save all types of fabric softener that are not recommended from an environmental point of view anyway.

However, you can reduce the time that you have hung up with laundry until the laundry is dry and the next one can be hung up and have spent the subsequent ironing by approx. 90%. In this way it is possible to do the weekly laundry of a family of four in a single day, even with four-hour eco-washing programs. You need a maximum of two nights if you do not have a chance during the day to change the washes between the devices.

If you belong to the households where the washing machine runs every day, this is an extremely big win for you.

Bedroom

The bedroom is usually the room in which the wardrobe is located.

Here the 5S action is used as a method. And it is not very obvious that processes are taking place that are worth taking a closer look at!

After all, the main task of a bedroom is to give us a space where we can relax and unwind. So the main purpose is sleeping as such.

Many people are prone to sleep problems these days. They fall asleep badly, roll around in bed for hours on end and find no rest due to the carousel of thoughts. In the middle of the night you wake up, your thoughts keep turning. The next morning the alarm clock rings, you press the snooze button until you can't get out of bed until you get up.

That does not have to be the case and therefore a process assessment, including the so-called value stream analysis, comes first.

The goal is for you to recover, that the night is used for sleeping instead of brooding, and that you can wake up to the day full of vigor and anticipation.

Practical instructions

The best way to start the 5S campaign is with the floor space and the storage space of various cupboards and dressers. Bedside tables are often a overloaded stain too. Put all things on the bed or a particularly large chest of drawers and sort them out. Which things do you really need and which of the required things actually have their place in the bedroom? Often numerous things accumulate here that have lost nothing there.

It's best to dedicate a day of your own to the wardrobe. Here it makes sense to divide the clothing into three stacks:

1. Will be kept

2. Can be sold second hand

3. Can be donated.

Do not have any illusions that worn clothing will still bring in a great deal of money. Fashion is a seasonal business - what was wearable last summer can be out of fashion a year later. Similar to art, you can only earn as much from second-hand clothing as someone else is willing to pay for it. In most cases, it doesn't matter how expensive things were when you bought them. Of course, there are exceptions - high-quality branded fashion will always be able to be sold well, but even here only at a fraction of the original price.

Then think about the concept of your wardrobe. It has proven useful to work with many drawers. There you fold the laundry so that it is placed upright in the drawers. In this way you save a lot of space, because now the complete cabinet depth is used and also in terms of height, much more clothes fit in the cabinet than with the classic clothing stacks. Another advantage of this method is that you no longer automatically only wear the top "favorite pieces", but can reach all parts at any time with one hand.

Also think of the one form of waste "unnecessary transportation". Keep the walkways short and sort the clothes in the closet so that when you choose a new outfit you don't have to walk across the entire bedroom three times to have all the pieces together.

If you have a dry cellar or attic, you may also be able to temporarily store seasonal goods there. So you don't have to store your ski pants next to your summer dress in your closet and you have more space.

Good sleep

Athletes know the feeling of "flow". Likewise, children who, completely immersed in their play world, skillfully ignore all of the parents' speeches. If you are so busy with a thing that you have experienced an euphoric elation afterwards, you want to repeat this moment over and over again.

Imagine that this is also possible with daily sleep! Instead of wallowing in bed frustratingly one night at a time, you could sleep soundly and then wake up in the morning with a feeling of vigor and joy. And get up!

Good sleep hygiene also includes a positive morning routine.

Now consider your "sleep process", ie the sleep routine in detail. Write down exactly when you usually go to bed, what you did in the two hours before, when you plan to get up. Then write down when the alarm should ring, whether you will actually get up at this point and how you will start the day. What exactly do you do in the hour after getting up?

You will find numerous tips on the Internet on how to practice healthy sleep hygiene. No more electronic media in the hour before falling asleep. No heavy food, no alcohol. Ensure good ventilation, low room temperature and noise reduction while sleeping.

For married couples, this can certainly raise the question of separate bedrooms. Women in particular often suffer from snoring partners and thus lose a lot of restful sleep. Talk to your partner about any prejudices about separate bedrooms! Many couples have different sleeping needs, and women usually sleep much better when they spend the night separately. The dilemma here lies in the fact that men often sleep better when there is a partner next to them. Talk to your partner and think again about Maslow and the different and individual needs of each individual.

There are just as many tips and hints for the morning routine after getting up on the Internet. I can highly recommend the book *The Miracle Morning* by Hal Elrod. It describes in a very practical way how you can start the day satisfied and full of energy every morning with a simple but highly efficient method. To do this, he takes six steps, the Life S.A.V.E.R.S. with which you can get up one hour earlier than usual and "change your life" during that one hour.

Elrod does not explicitly refer to the method of lean management, but ultimately the added value of your morning work is also questioned here. It is also motivating that there is a "Companion Planner" for his book, a workbook that helps you to implement the routine step by step.

Children's room

Since you bought this book, I assume that at least one child is - or will be - part of your life.

With children it is again important to be aware that everyone has their own needs and desires. Especially when it comes to order, children have a completely different sense of order than adults. How often do parents complain about the supposed disorder in the children's room, while the children know exactly where which building block on the floor belongs, which stickers from the collection absolutely have to be kept and which pictures they simply have not yet finished and are therefore being kept.

Of course, it is important to offer children certain basic rules and structures. Consistent example is the most effective method here. Check yourself how you deal with order in the kitchen, basement, bathroom.

Even today, children are often not involved in household chores to the extent that would be acceptable for them. The division of tasks in the household very often remains with the parents, and more often with one person.

When sorting things out, however, children have a worse reputation than is real. Children are very good at sorting things out, since here the wishes of the parents collide with those of the children.

Practical instructions

You start with a thorough 5S campaign in the children's room. However, make sure that your child is there and give them the decision-making authority in their hands, what things should be kept and what can be sorted out. Get rid of values - a 200-Dollar model ship that was once a gift from Santa Claus, but which has never been played with, can be sorted out!

But also teach your child that they should only keep things that they really enjoy. It doesn't have to keep gifts from aunts, uncles, or grandparents just because they were gifts. You should also ignore the price. Especially when it comes to Christmas gifts, you find yourself in a moral dilemma. A particularly expensive Christmas gift may have been financially at your limit - for your child it was just a (sometimes even undesirable) gift from Santa Claus.

Then choose the right places for the remaining toys. "Every piece has its place" can also be inquired in children with "Where does this part live?"

The subsequent labeling of the various boxes and containers is particularly popular with children. Paint labels, print symbols, or think with children who can already read what terms you can use to label the places. The offspring is also proud to be able to take the labeling device in their own hands, and it is not uncommon for them to label even the smallest box with total dedication.

Mother's help

Next, you should prepare the children for the KANBAN meeting and inform them that the household chores will be redistributed at the next family meeting (see also: Kitchen section). Of course, this works best with children from preschool age, but it also makes sense from this age.

The best way to do this is as follows: each family member receives a white sheet and a pen. Now note and write down: which tasks do I do myself in the household? A simple question with a big impact. Make sure that even the smallest detail is recorded here. Making beds, filling up the soap in the bathroom, cooking, sweeping the floor, making the balcony plants ready for wintertime, watering the flowers, clearing out the dishwasher, filling up the storage jars ... The list will certainly be very long for one or the other. In many families it is still the case that 80% of the work is usually done by one person, the partner takes over 15% and the children often only 5%.

In order to live in an equal and happy family, equality must take place here. At this point, I simply assume that both parents have a certain job. Of course, it makes a big difference whether your profession is housewife or home-maker per se. In my opinion an absolutely full and underestimated full time job! But then the starting situation is completely different from that described here.

Then summarize the tasks and check how they could be distributed in the future. Depending on the age of the children, they should cover 10 to 20% of the total effort. You can help with tablecloths or take away old glass or paper waste.

Guest room

If you're the lucky owner of a guest room, you probably won't see a lot of things here. At least you shouldn't. A guest room serves to accommodate guests and is not an alternative to the storage room, ironing room or a second workshop.

Walk around the room with a watchful eye and critically examine whether these things really belong here or whether anything should be sorted out. A larger 5S campaign is not even necessary in most cases. If so, that would be the first step.

Focus your attention here on the processes that are important when you receive guests. Are you planning visits in time? Enter the dates on your KANBAN board. This way you know at least 14 days in advance when to expect guests.

Dress up the room nicely, get fresh flowers on the day of arrival, and try to provide guests with a space to relax. You also don't want to spend the night with friends in the ironing room or literally feel pushed onto the siding in the storage room.

But you don't have to make excessive efforts. Fresh flowers, fresh bed linen and vacuumed the room - there are little things that make a guest feel good!

Change the bed linen immediately after departure - not before the next guest is expected. Wash, dry and then make the bed. Doing these steps after your visit will save you a lot of stress instead of doing everything the day before new guests arrive.

Home-Office / Workspace

The most important process that accompanies you at home is working as such. You want to work efficiently and not be distracted by hundreds of other, private, activities. To do this, it is important that you only have the things you need to work.

If you share the workplace, this is all the more important since one should not be distracted from the other's things and also does not want to.

Practical instructions

As part of a 5S campaign, first check whether there are really only things in the home office that actually belong here.

You should keep all kinds of private documents in a separate cupboard or at least a compartment. Folders in which you can lay loose sheets have worked well here so that you can collect and edit them later.

You should also consider the motto *less is more* when it comes to decorative items. This is particularly important in the case of shared workplaces, since every person has a different need for order.

Just imagine when setting up that you would share one of the new mobile workplaces in an open-plan office that are not assigned to a permanent employee. At first, this may seem strange and you still feel uncomfortable - I often hear the argument that the workplace then appears so impersonal. However, if you ask furnishing consultants or Feng Shui experts, they recommend placing green plants at the workplace instead. However, these should really be taken care of, because nothing lowers the efficiency when working as much as a depressing, half-dying, dried office plant!

Streams

Now look at your processes: which tools do you need to work? Is the computer functional or should it be urgently updated? Are all office supplies working or is something missing? Try to use good quality products, no cheap pens that write ugly, no bad paper to print on.

How do you start your day-to-day work? Check your previous work routine and improve it if necessary. Numerous guides can of course help you with this. A book that I can recommend to you as a Professional Organizer is *Getting things done* by David Allen – it is a must-read for Professional Organizers. Allen describes in a very detailed and descriptive manner how you can keep track of things, especially with regard to paper documents and notes, but also in terms of planning, in terms of appointments and activities, and not get bogged down. Using his own method, he describes how you can efficiently process, sort and file documents - whether professional or private.

An extremely important point that I would like to draw out is the topic of the Zero Inbox: it is feasible to raise the inbox, whether electronic or paper-based, to such a low level that you actually have no or very, very few messages in the inbox have to keep.

I personally usually have four to five messages in my inbox. These are things that I still have to do, but that take more than two minutes to get them done. In this way you can start working at the beginning of your work without having to spend time searching and sorting.

In the home office, in particular, your focus should be on everything you do bringing you closer to your goal. Or serves to do your job. Process steps that are stopping you or that are not relevant for the fulfillment of your tasks should be checked and, if necessary, changed or deleted.

Establish routines and procedures for effective work and you will see that you will soon be able to work more productively in the home office than at the actual office workstation. Of course, all of these tips also depend on the activity you are performing. A taxi driver will certainly won't work more effectively in the home office because he has to drive a car. Just pay attention to your streams!

Basement

Now it's time to go from the living area into the basement. It usually becomes literally dark. You can encounter a lot in the basement.

It is important here that the basement receives a basic order and has not been delivered.

If you want to find a happy and satisfied family at home, you need a solid foundation. From a psychological perspective, you would now be advised that you cannot build a solid foundation on a shaky foundation. Your house will stand like a spongy rubble field and you will be constantly trying to balance this shaky and unstable feeling.

That is why a tidy basement can create miracles and form a stable basis for a happy family life.

Practical instructions

The 5S campaign in the basement is usually one of the larger cleanups. It is best to take a whole day for this and plan to actually spend this day only with mucking out and sorting out. No ironing in between, no shopping, no car washing. Concentrate fully on the 5S campaign and you will be completely done with it after one or a maximum of two days (i.e. a whole weekend).

When you have completed step 1, the sorting, you should then pay attention to step 4, the standardization. Maybe it's time to put a shadow board above the workbench? Or somewhere on the wall in the basement, only the necessary space has to be available.

Also label the toolboxes - if you have a lot of leisure, you can label the individual screw, dowel and small parts assortment boxes.

Make sure that all tools have their fixed place and do not have to be cleared to reach it. This is necessary so that you have the tools at hand *Just In Time* - exactly when you need them. Especially when it comes to tools, there is often an urgent need when a tool is needed, and who wants to search and clear around for a long time before you can use the tool that you urgently need!

In some households there are other rooms in the basement such as a hobby room or a private gym. Therefore, these spaces can be considered as equivalent:

Hobby room / musician's room / gym / crafts / garage

All these rooms have in common that they are designed for leisure activities. Whether you are screwing on your classic car in the garage, doing something in the hobby cellar, making music with your hobby band in the music room ...

You see: here are the rules. *Every piece has its place* and *like to like*.

Practical instructions

Use the 5S method to sort out vigorously and purposefully and decide which leisure activities you still practice. Many hobbies are lost over time, new jobs are added.

Things that are often stored here are things for vacation. Surf boards and sand toys are stored here for beach holidays, sturdy hiking boots and backpacks for holidays in the mountains and a wide range of horse gear and riding accessories for holidays on the riding stable.

Then take a close look at this holiday process: when do you actually start planning your holiday? Are you booking last-minute trips for fun or because you missed the early planning? When do you submit your vacation planning to your employer and how flexible can you make these days? Most workers should know by the end of the year when they want to take vacation the following year. Save yourself the stress of not planning your vacation until the days between Christmas and New Year. A perfect month to plan vacations is October, for example. There is still enough time until the end of the year, but if you take a closer look, nothing changes between October and December from a purely planning point of view. Except that you miss out all early bird discounts because you adhere to the belief that only over-organized people book vacations so early.

Be smart and use October! At this point, all school holidays are already available, the travel providers, campsites and hotels offer you good early bird prices and you don't have the feeling that you have to make decisions under time pressure and stress. Take the whole four weeks in October to do some cozy research in the evening, think about it and then distribute the vacation days. You can then still wait until mid-November to hand in the delivery, giving yourself another two weeks to consider.

But how do you like the idea of literally knowing where you're going in December, and above all: knowing that you won't have to rush and, in a hurry, plan the vacation days between the years and decide accordingly when to go where. No, you can enjoy this time and instead enjoy the days off that await you after Christmas.

Extra topic: the car

Another process that is inevitably associated with vacationing is owning a car. Most readers will have at least one car in the garage, in front of the house, in the driveway. As a family, you will also need a relatively large car. But here, too, it is important to weigh realistically and constructively.

An example:

You have two children and spend three weeks at a campsite in Spain every summer. You have 2000 km of travel in front of you, a large tent with you - or maybe you can rent a chic mobile home - and numerous things you need with children on a typical summer vacation. You need space for it and definitely a big car.

Of course, it was previously out of the question to buy a correspondingly large car. Whether as a leased company car, as a used car or possibly as a new model. There are numerous variants, but you can turn it as you like: a large car is much more expensive than a smaller car.

So, do the math, summarize how often in the year you actually have to take up the space that the big car offers you. In 80% of the families, this enormous amount of space is actually only needed for this one-year vacation. For a maximum of one week of ski vacation during the winter holidays. The total should not exceed four weeks here.

Now we assume purely fictitious, you also lived in a larger city, occasionally have parking problems with the big car and also pay a correspondingly high vehicle tax. For everyday use, use public transport, walk or cycle. Which makes more sense from an ecological perspective anyway.

Conversely, this would mean that you would use the large car to full capacity for four weeks, but a smaller car would be sufficient for 48 weeks a year.

So, you can ask yourself: doesn't it make much more sense to own or lease a smaller car and to borrow a correspondingly large car for these four, sometimes only three or two weeks a year?

Always think needs-based! Keep the process of car use *lean*. Drive the car yourself that meets 80 or 90% of your needs and tailor the requirements accordingly. The last 10-20% is a rented car completely sufficient. Just skip the big vacation once - in one fell swoop, your entire bill no longer works.

Just In Time - get the car exactly when you need it. Don't waste time or money by over-fulfilling the requirements.

You can also compare the topics of *efficiency and effectiveness* here. Of course, you can take a large sprinter to the supermarket to buy a pack of flour and a bottle of milk. This is effective because you can do the job. It would be efficient to drive a small scooter, since exactly one pack of flour and a bottle of milk fit in its trunk.

Hobbies in general

The main problem for most people here is the assumption that one could try some hobbies again later than before. In most cases this is a fallacy - and you know it too. Rather, it is about letting go of once loved things and admitting that you will no longer take up this or that hobby.

Just be aware of this fact, be self-disciplined (remember, that was the 5th S of the 5S method) and critically question which hobbies you will actually ever tackle again. Sometimes the materials are simply out of date and can no longer be used. Things from the hobby area can often still be exchanged at reasonable prices or equivalent articles can be exchanged.

If you have clarity in this area, you can look forward to the newly gained feeling of freedom, because you no longer have to worry about one-off hobbies.

Garden

Let us turn to the last "room" in this book, if it exists in your house or apartment. How to apply lean principles in a garden, balcony or patio?

The garden in general is a symbol for us as a place of relaxation. We can retreat here when the stress has gained the upper hand, when we need rest or simply to be able to enjoy nature in all its glory.

Practical instructions

At the beginning there is also a sorting out of all unnecessary things using the 5S method. Check which tools are still functional, what should be repaired and what can no longer be used.

You can also rethink your planting - are there plants that do not thrive well, maybe they need to change location?

And then turn to the real task of this place:

Use your garden or balcony as a place of rest to reflect relaxed about your previous life. Think about Maslow and its pyramid of needs or question the process changes that have been implemented so far. Don't forget that in the spirit of KAIZEN your personal attitude is required. The lean concept implies an attitude to life that sees lifelong learning as the basis.

Think of your life as a big apple tree. Now stand next to it and take a close look - some branches carry good and many apples, others are rather stunted or even dead.

What have you done in the past to make this tree, your tree of life, look like this? There were times when the tree was particularly well looked after. But there were also moments when a radical step back was necessary or the years when you might not have cared about growth and wellbeing at all.

Take a look back in time! In peace and calm.

Then - and this is the important core of the lean philosophy: think about how your tree should continue to grow! How should it develop, what are your goals and wishes?

The most important step is now: submit concrete measures that lead to an improvement! Use the power of visualization - this is an incredibly effective tool. You will find numerous tips and tricks on this individual topic on the Internet and in specialist books.

It is a matter of imagining the target state down to the last detail.

In our example, a powerful, old, large apple tree. With a mighty, protective treetop and many delicious, wonderful apples. In spring you can enjoy the apple blossom, in autumn the rich harvest. Smell the scent of apple blossoms, hear the buzz of the bees in spring. Imagine sitting under your tree with a freshly picked apple in the fall. See yourself standing in the kitchen and peeling the apples - and taste the juicy apple pie that you baked from the first harvest!

You immediately know that you have to have a fruit tree cut or have it done at least once a year in order to let this tree unfold to its full splendor. You could do a fruit tree pruning course. You may have to deal with the topic of pests (because you noticed a few wormholes when you peeled the apples) and learn what you can do about them and how to recognize them at an early stage. You need to know what you're going to do with the harvest - do you want to produce apple juice or maybe even a pleasant fruit brandy? Do you know a distillery that can do this work for you? If not, you have to search for it.

The more detailed you imagine your goals, the clearer you will know which steps you have to take next in order to achieve this goal in the long term.

Use the power of visualization for your life goals and your personal needs.

Sometimes you also notice at this point that your partner's wishes do not match or no longer match your own wishes. At this point you should look for a third conversation partner who can help you here. See this external interlocutor as the professional landscape gardener who can offer you the right solution for unknown pests.

Finally, imagine the relief and joy that you will feel when your apple tree already bears the fruits of your efforts the next year!

You have now reached the end of your little trip through your family home. If you miss a room or a special place then you certainly have enough imagination which of the lean methods can be used there according to the previous descriptions.

4

Summary

*Organization isn't about perfection;
it's about efficiency,
reducing stress and clutter,
saving time and money and
improving your
overall quality of life.*

Christina Scalise

Congratulations! You have read the most important basics of lean management for your family and have perhaps already implemented one or the other.

Perhaps you also asked yourself between the individual chapters what is the difference between lean and good organization?

It's simple: imagine a well-organized wardrobe. Every piece of clothing is in its place, everything is neatly folded and ready to be worn. Nevertheless, you will never wear 80% of the clothes, or you will only wear them very rarely. You may be organized at this point, but absolutely unprofitable and wasteful of resources, space, and ultimately money.

It is also not a question of implementing all the methods listed here as quickly as possible. Some things can even be completely destructive for you. Under no circumstances put yourself under stress, or consider the processes mentioned in this book as set!

I repeat the *core idea* of lean management:

„Lean Management is a way to do more and more with less and less - less human effort, less equipment, less time, and less space - while coming closer and closer to providing customers exactly what they want.

Lean is founded on the concept of continuous and incremental improvements on product and process while eliminating redundant activities."

Source: Wikipedia
(https://en.wikipedia.org/wiki/Lean_manufacturing)

The most important principles in a nutshell

The *value* of *streams*

KANBAN – Visualization and planning

KAIZEN – the Continuous Improvement Process CIP

MUDA – the 7 forms of *waste*

5S – muck and clear out sustainably

HADOME – The 5 Why?'s

HANSEI – Reflection with Maslows hierarchy of needs

JIT „*Just in Time*" – the 5 R's

PULL – Needs-based fulfillment

If you consistently use one of the methods or one of the principles mentioned, stress and chaos in your family life will slowly but surely disappear.

Always focus on the processes you can find in your household. Imagine your family as a gigantic factory where numerous needs have to be met. Are all these needs met? If not, where can you start to achieve step by step what is important to each individual family member in life?

And celebrate your success! You can congratulate yourself, do yourself something good - you have done great things once you have made an improvement!

Lean is supposed to be fun, not compulsive and serve your own improvement. You will literally enjoy it when your family's mood changes from frustration to *flow*. Treat yourself and your loved ones to something beautiful and be proud of the changes that have done so much good that YOU have done!

102

Would you like to get started, but would you like to have a basic plan of when and how best to start?

In the next chapter you will receive an exemplary implementation plan that can guide you to start with the first lean steps.

The plan is structured so that you can bring about visible changes in the first three months. The really big, long-term results are achieved after an average of one year.

5

One year living LEAN

Knowing is not enough, we must apply.
Willing is not enough, we must do.

Bruce Lee

The big picture

This book is designed to help you save more time and money at the same time.

If you implement LEAN for a year, you can assume that you will end up with at least 30% more time per day and that your earnings will have increased by at least 30%.

Of course, there can be no guarantee, because ultimately, like so much, depends on your own self-discipline and cooperation. However, if you want to live a fulfilling life instead of a frustrated life, you can do that in the next twelve months.

You can start with your personal LEAN year at any time - I recommend choosing a beginning of the month for the sake of simplicity. You can (and should!) shorten or extend the suggestions and ideas, depending on how it fits your life situation and circumstances.

Each month is assigned a focus topic, which you can of course vary freely. The present months are a logical example. I deliberately put the topic at the beginning, so that you can briefly skim through the months and assigned topics at the beginning in order to finally assess whether the order should be arranged differently for you from the outset. However, this order is based on years of experience, so you can rest assured.

I hope you enjoy this wonderful year of your family life!

1st month - HANSEI

Topic of this month: HANSEI – Reflection with Maslow

Start your personal year with a month of reflection. You and your family should consciously take a whole month to reflect, summarize and compile. Buy a nice empty book for it, maybe even a particularly appealing pen, and write down the thoughts that follow. Place the book in a place where it can be reached by any family member at any time.

Give each member time for themselves, time to think about it for themselves.

Schedule family reunions once a week for this month to share results and summarize at the end of the month.

Always begin with the future

How did you imagine life as a family? Where do you see yourself in five years, where in ten? How do your children want to live, what hobbies and leisure activities do you want to do or try out together? Are there heart wishes or projects that you have put off so far or that you have planned for the future?

It is important here to consider each individual family member as an individual, but also the big picture, to include wishes as a family.

Use the complete power of thought, visualization! Imagine this future in as much detail as possible. How will you feel when you have achieved these goals? How will it taste, smell? (You may dream of a house in Southern France - close your eyes and smell the lavender from your own garden, see the pine trees right in front of you and taste the aromatic Camembert cheese and a glass of red wine).

What goals do you want to achieve in the family using LEAN?

Reflect the present

Where are you now? What have you achieved so far and how are you doing in the current situation? Are you satisfied, do you want improvements? What are your biggest construction sites as a family, what habits or personal settings do you want to work on, what characteristics do you like?

Do you know about the wishes and needs of your family members? Does everyone know how the other is doing?

Finish with the past

What brought you this far? What paths have you taken to get where you are now? Did you have rituals, routines, habits that helped you? Or who may have hindered you?

Are there issues from the past that you should capture and close? In rare cases, the support of a life coach or a trustworthy person can be advisable.

Make a summary and write down your plans

Now write down as precisely as possible your goals and wishes that you have worked out this month. What processes do you want to change, what is your greatest suffering and what are the most important issues that you want to tackle together as a family, but also as individuals?

Then make an appointment for yourself and your family in six months! Usually the time between Christmas and New Year's and the summer holidays is the best time for these following reflection weeks or days.

Result

Now you know where your biggest weak spots are, where you have equally found the greatest potential and what to do in the coming months.

2nd month - 5S

Topic of this month: 5S

This month you are dedicating yourself to a large-scale 5S campaign.

Take four weekends for a big mucking out program.

Make a mucking-out plan

Take a large sheet of paper (flipchart sheets are best) and write down all the spaces and places you always wanted to muck out. Expect that - if you work concentrated - you will need an average of one day for one room.

Decide which rooms will get first priority for this month and get started!

The 5 steps in a brief overview

Again, for a brief summary, here are the 5 steps in detail:

Step 1: SEIRI - sort out

Step 2: SEITON – set in order

Step 3: SEISO - shine

Step 4: SEIKETSU - standardize

Step 5: SHITSUKE – sustain / self-discipline

Follow these 5 steps as in the first part of the book described and select the rooms in which it seems most urgent to you. You will probably have addressed this in the first month!

Take your time, but do not postpone the necessary actions! Perseverance is the magic word here. If you need motivational aids, get motivating postcards to remind you of them. Search the internet for funny sayings, a task that young people like to take on too!

Agree on who will then take care of the disposal of things. It has been proven that one partner is responsible for the transport or organization of the bulky waste and the other is responsible for the sale and donation of the good used items.

Finally, plan which rooms you want to tackle in half a year, because then the topic 5S is again on the annual plan.

Result

Freedom and less ballast through junk and unpleasant objects in the house. You only surround yourself with things that you and your family like and that are good for you.

3rd month - KANBAN

Topic of this month: Visualization with KANBAN

After the first two months of reflection and decluttering, it's now the time for future planning.

Make an own KANBAN-Board

To create a KANBAN board, you need a blackboard, a whiteboard, a large varnished board - a way to attach or record a weekly schedule and, if necessary, collect other documents related to family planning (invitation cards, event notices, etc.).

In the first part of the book you will find some practical examples for KANBAN boards.

If you have the board, define the associated space. Mostly the entrance area or the kitchen are suitable, in some households (especially with an open kitchen) the living room can also be the best place for this. It is important that all family members have access to it at all times.

Then you set a first date on which you as a family can fundamentally determine what should be shown on the KANBAN board.

A fourteen-day weekly schedule with fixed appointments, household chores and birthdays or other events have proven their worth. You can find out more about this in the corresponding chapter in the first part of this book.

After the first appointment, you decide when to schedule the following appointment. Here, too, a weekly, short meeting of a maximum of 15 minutes is appropriate. Sunday evenings are very suitable, as this means that the weekly planning does not take place until Monday morning and you also know on Monday mornings what you want to cook for the rest of the week, have to shop, etc. As a small detail, you should pay particular attention to this when planning your meal. Make sure that you include the Monday of the new week in the planning - otherwise you risk a stressful Monday as you will then no longer have enough food at home. But this is just a very detailed note on the side. Still, this is an important point because with a well-thought-out meal plan, you can greatly reduce food waste. You can deliberately plan meals, the rest of which you can take to school the next day or work as a snack.

As you noticed in the previous months, it is important that you do not focus on several changes at the same time. Don't try to change too much at once! The focus for the third month lies only in these weekly meetings and in the purchase and establishment of the KANBAN board.

Result

You slow down your everyday life immensely, but at the same time optimize planning. Missed appointments are a thing of the past. You save costs because you have introduced a meal plan and minimize food waste in the household.

4th month - Streams

Topic of this month: The value of streams

Since you have been dealing with the LEAN topic for a quarter and have tackled the basic things, you can now devote yourself to the actually most important core of lean management:

the streams.

Take the time to collect and write down the absolutely most annoying, time-consuming, exhausting, and unpopular processes.

This can be washing clothes, shopping, cooking or cleaning. The process of tidying up and keeping order is also at the top of the list. Just as completing the tax return or filing all the paper documents, ergo doing the inbox.

Record the processes like a long thread.

Wherever you find bottlenecks, let the thread get tangled up in a small ball. Then measure the time from one ball to the next and also the time the process is in the wrapped ball.

The dirty shirt

You take off a shirt in the evening that needs to be washed. Your thread begins. You put the shirt on the chair in front of your bed, the first ball in the thread. The shirt will be there for five days until you take it and throw it in the laundry basket in the bathroom. Here the thread has its next skein, the shirt remains in the basket for another six days until it continues to follow the thread and finds its way into the washing machine. The washing takes three hours, so a very small ball. Then the shirt in the finished laundry waits another half a day until you come back from work and hang the laundry on the clothesline. The shirt hangs on the clothesline, a larger ball, for another two days. Then you take it down and put it with all the other laundry in a laundry basket that needs to be sorted. This process, the way from one ball to the other, takes another 30 minutes. After a busy day and eight hours of waiting, you finally decide to sort the laundry and put the shirt back in the closet. You can calculate for yourself how long the process will take for you and how many shirts you would need to have in order to have enough fresh laundry available.

Clean up the stream

You remember that every step in a process should include a value-adding component. You should bring all steps closer to the actual goal, and do it as efficiently as possible.

The new stream

You take off the shirt in the evening and immediately put it in the bathroom for other dirty laundry. You can wash it after three days at the latest - if you have only collected a little dirty laundry, it does not matter, because most washing machines now have a short program that is often the most economical in terms of ecology and requires little laundry. The washing process is then reduced to one hour. Invest the money in an energy saving dryer! And as soon as the laundry is ready, put it in the dryer. For delicate clothes, drying on the clothesline can still make sense, then this process takes two days longer on the spot. If you have a dryer in the evening, when you get home from work, take the shirt, fold it up and put it back in the closet.

The process is dramatically shortened, the thread only contains three skeins (dirty laundry basket, washing, drying) and you also save a large amount of clothing, since the shirt is back in place on the fourth day.

General procedure

This month dedicate yourself to the main processes that you would like to improve. Write them down and consider which specific steps you have to take in order to gain more value in the process and whether all previous steps were really necessary to achieve the corresponding goal.

For the beginning and this month, one to a maximum of three processes should suffice. Implementing changes is always an obstacle for people and it takes at least 30 days to establish new routines!

Result

This month, you were able to save time and costs by turning to the most important long and expensive processes and redesigning them in lean steps.

5th month - KAIZEN

Topic of this month: KAIZEN and CIP

The fifth month is all about the CIP - the Continuous Improvement Process.

This point lends itself seamlessly to viewing the past three months.

You take a closer look at whether the topics that you initiated from the second to the fourth month have proven their worth, or whether there is room for improvement.

A first review

In the second month you had mucked out - you may now notice things at one point or another in your house that you did not want to give up two months ago, but would now like to part with. It is important: do not tackle any new rooms or places that you have not yet cleared out in the second month! Only refer to the places and things already processed!

In the third month you had introduced and established the KANBAN board. Has it worked well with it? Do the weekly KANBAN meetings take place at the most convenient time for you? Is the board used and if not, why or at which points not? What could be optimized, improved here?

Last but not least, you had specifically selected one or three processes that you wanted to improve. Did this work or did a new ball of thread unexpectedly appear elsewhere in the process thread?

Examine and question critically the ideas and actions implemented so far and consider which ones could be made even more efficient. Remember that while it is effective to light a candle with a flame thrower, it would be efficient if you just used a match.

Result

You have learned to differentiate between effectiveness and efficiency. True to the motto "lifelong learning" you are ready to accept new things and to continuously improve.

6th month - Success

Topic of this month: celebrate your successes

An equally important and decisive moment if you want to live LEAN: Be aware of what you have achieved so far and celebrate your success!

Pat yourself on the back of what you have achieved so far, enjoy the new attitude to life that has already set in and simply enjoy life.

If you introduce the lean methods in companies as a management consultant, a final presentation will take place at the end of the implementation, which in some consulting companies is also colloquially referred to as the "lean festival". In this presentation, the previous successes are celebrated and celebrated.

Result

You focus on the saying "business before pleasure" and, with all optimization and improvements, do not forget that overcome challenges can be celebrated. You feel proud and confident; your energy level has increased.

7th month - HANSEI II

Topic of this month: HANSEI – repetition

Half a year of LEAN is now behind you and you have recognized the most important principles and applied methods.

This month you turn to reflection again.

Reflect on what you have achieved so far

Perhaps you have had no time in the past six months, or you could take a look from time to time: take the book in which you wrote down in the first month what goals and wishes you defined as family and as individuals had.

It's a little easier this time.

You check which of the wishes have already been fulfilled, which have had difficulties and which may not have been necessary. Maybe new requests have also been added?

Check it off, take notes - do what you like best. It is enough if you only check this half-year overview.

In another half a year you can completely redefine the goals and wishes - this month, however, the focus is on the pure review of the previously noted wishes.

Result

You have a current status regarding the (non) achievement of your previous wishes and goals and were able to adapt and update them accordingly.

8th month - 5S II

Topic of this month: 5S - repetition

You also start the second round with another 5S action.

Mocking out part 2

With enough distance from the last big ditching campaign, this month you take on the second part of the rooms that you have not yet tackled.

If you have already completely cleaned out all rooms in the second month, use this eighth month to repeat the action. Most of the time you will find numerous objects that appeared to you six months ago to be unchangeable, from which you would now like to separate.

In the next few years, this month can also take a shorter period and be spread over the entire year. Once you have thoroughly cleared out and ensure that no such quantities of things accumulate in the future, you will no longer need two months a year to deal with remedial actions.

Result

Depending on the size of your household, the first complete littering campaign has now ended. There are only things in your household that make you happy and that delight your heart.

9th month - Streams II

Topic of this month: Streams - repetition

In the ninth month of your personal LEAN year, consider the processes again.

New streams

This month, too, focus on processes that you have not yet considered or have not considered sufficiently.

Again, it makes sense to limit yourself to a few processes.

Check which streams are not yet running smoothly or select those that you have noticed in the meantime. You can distribute the few remaining processes to be checked over the next few months.

Result

Most of the processes in your family should now be lean and add value. You have achieved optimum time and cost savings and see things much more clearly than a year ago.

10th month - KAIZEN II

Topic of this month: KAIZEN - repetition

The last quarter of your first LEAN year is approaching and you are turning one last time specifically and consciously to the CIP - the continuous improvement process.

Weak spots

Check: can you find weak spots or vulnerabilities in the previous optimizations? Are there processes or things that you or another family member does not feel comfortable with? Is there anything that could be improved?

Make yourself aware this month that the CIP will also be a permanent, incidental tool of your LEAN toolbox in the future, that you should no longer limit yourself to individual months or weeks, but anchor it in your philosophy every day.

Result

You have developed a feeling for looking at things from a different perspective. You no longer feel like a constant optimizer, but have developed a calm inner attitude based on the motto "lifelong learning".

11th month - MUDA

Topic of this month: MUDA and the 7 forms of waste

The penultimate month of your LEAN year now turns to the 7 forms of waste.

In the past weeks and months, you have certainly been subconsciously or consciously paying attention to the individual forms of waste. At this point we summarize them again:

The 7 forms of waste in an overview

1. Overproduction
2. Inventory
3. Correction and defects
4. Waiting
5. Unnecessary transport
6. Unnecessary movement
7. Overprocessing

Try to identify and eliminate the possible forms of waste in your household. The best way to do this is to focus on both the processes and the individual rooms. You can find stocks quickly, for example, by a simple house inspection, waiting times and unnecessary transport by looking closely at your streams.

Since you have already worked intensively on and improved some processes, this month you can actually concentrate on the fine details or on processes that you have not yet had a direct eye on.

In the area of waste from an ecological point of view, pay particular attention to the subject areas of kitchen and food, as well as clothing and accessories.

Result

You have improved your carbon footprint and also saved time, money and food. You have learned that you can save such things without having to forego comfort or luxury, but consciously saved what was already unnecessary or too much.

12th month   -   Success

Topic of this month: celebrate your successes!

You finally did it and you can congratulate yourself and your family!

Organize a party, invite friends and relatives and celebrate your great success!

Enjoy what you have achieved and treat yourself to the rewards you deserve!

Result

After one year of LEAN, you should have achieved one goal: a more fulfilling and relaxed life. You now know where you are and what the goals of each family member are.

The household budget is more relaxed, because not only have you learned to pay attention, but you have uncovered numerous other forms of waste in your household.

In that one year you have achieved a whole new level of clarity about how you want to live; you have separated yourself from nervous and time-consuming things and activities; you are financially in a better situation than before and the most important thing:

You understood that all of these LEAN methods and tools could help you live a better life without having to dispense something important or loved!

And although you have been able to improve a lot, you are aware that lifelong learning has also increased in value in the area of your family life. You are curious and interested and look forward to new ideas and suggestions for improvement every day that you would never have thought of before.

Your life philosophy has changed, you are able to think "slim" and in you only concentrate on the things that create value.

Now take a careful look at the photos you took at the beginning of your personal LEAN year! Enjoy the success - you may not even be able to believe some of the situations shown in the pictures.

124

Prospect

At this point there's only one thing left to say:

Go on like that!

You can be proud of yourself, proud that you were able and wanted to experience so much.

I would hope that from now on your life will feel easier and freer and that together with me you could discover the joys of lean management in the household.

If you liked this book, I would be delighted if you tell your friends and buddies about it, if you share your successes or send me a message!

I am particularly pleased that I was able to be part of this very personal journey for you and I wish you a life shaped by love, happiness and fulfillment.

5

Motivating quotes

Life itself is a quotation.

Jorge Louis Borges

It is always easier with support. Here you will find a small collection of motivational sayings and quotes that you can use as food for thought or maybe just to make you smile.

I cannot say whether things get better if we change; what I can say is that they must change if they are to get better. – Georg Christoph Lichtenberg

Don't wait. The time will never be just right. – Napoleon Hill

The best time to plant a tree was twenty years ago. The second best time is now. – Chinese proverb

Some people don't like change. But you need to embrace change if the alternative is disaster. – Elon Musk

The slowest, who just doesn't lose sight of his goal, is still faster than the one who wanders around without a goal. – Gotthold Ephraim Lessing

One waits for time to change, the other grabs it and acts! – Dante Alighieri

A goal is a dream with a Deadline. — Napoleon Hill

I think that's the single best piece of advice: Constantly think about how you could be doing things better and questioning yourself. – Elon Musk

If you always do what you've always done, you'll always get what you've always got. – Henry Ford

Insanity is doing the same thing over and over again and expecting different results – Albert Einstein

It's never too late to be what you might have been. – George Eliot

When it is obvious that the goals cannot be reached, don't adjust the goals, adjust the action steps. – Confucius

Good things come to those who wait. But better things come to those who work for it. – Brian Tracy

You shouldn't do things differently just because they are different. They need to be better. – Elon Musk

It's not that we have a short time to live, but that we waste a lot of it. – Lucius Annaeus Seneca

Every man is guilty of all the good he did not do – Voltaire

Most people spend more time and energy going around problems than in trying to solve them. – Henry Ford

Lean is a term that is easy to memorize, but a complicated concept that is not immediately obvious. – Takahiro Fujimoto

I think it's possible for ordinary people to choose to be extraordinary. – Elon Musk

It's not because things are difficult that we do not dare; it's because we do not dare that they are difficult. – Lucius Annaeus Seneca

Learn to let go. That is the key to happiness. – Buddha

6

Literature

*Every man who knows how to read
has it in his power to magnify himself,
to multiply the ways in which he exists,
to make his life full, significant and interesting.*

Aldous Huxley

Lean Management

Lean Thinking: Womack, James P.; Jones, Daniel T. – Simon & Schuster UK

The Toyota Way: Liker, Jeffrey K. – McGraw-Hill

Professional Organising

The Life-Changing Magic of Tidying Up: Kondo, Marie – Ten Speed Press

Getting Things Done: Allen, David – Penguin Books

How to Simplify your life: Küstenmacher, Werner Tiki – McGraw-Hill Education

Martha Stewart's Homekeeping Handbook: Stewart, Martha – Clarkson Potter

Personal development

The Miracle Morning: the 6 Habits that will transform your life before 8 AM: Elrod, Hal – John Murray Learning

The Miracle Equation: Elrod, Hal – John Murray Learning

Rich Dad Poor Dad: Kiyosaki, Robert T. – Plata Publishing

The Yummy Mummy's Survival Guide: Fraser, Liz – HarperCollins

7

Thank you

There shall be an eternal summer
in the grateful heart.

Celia Thaxter

At this point I would like to thank all those who believe in me and who motivated me in such a troubled time.

First of all, I would like to thank my two children Kelvin and Kira - without you I would never have been able to write this book, because thanks to you I am sometimes a lovable mother, sometimes a fearsome mom-dragon. This family would not exist without you!

Special thanks also go to Florian – you told me the basics of my LEAN knowledge years ago. When I wrote this book, you were able to answer questions late in the evening and provide helpful tips if, once again, I did not see the forest for the trees - or rather, had lost my thread due to the streams.

I would also like to thank Carsten, who gave me the chance to made a movie of this content before the publication of the book and made it available digitally to all those who would rather briefly learn the contents of this book as an online course. In addition, this book would not have been finished so quickly, because from you, dear Carsten, I received one of the best literature tips of my life, you gave me the Miracle Morning!

Another thanks goes to my dear roommate Roland, who always provides me with sweet bits from the bakery when I have a literary writer's block or want to discuss one of my countless new ideas again. Thank you for your open ears, and for one of the most motivating quotes ever: Success has two letters – D O!

Not to be forgotten at this point are my dear business colleagues, above all Markus, the best painter on earth, who is always open to me and always good at advice, regardless of the situation! I would also like to thank Timo, my personal alternative practitioner, who always calms me down when I suffer from acute sagging or various fears of death as a self-confessed semi-hypochondriac. Your globules and your soothing words work wonders!

I would also like to thank you for your supportive, motivating and positive words, but also for justified reviews and advice: Beate B., Brigitta Z., Christian P., Claudia T., Georg N., Hajo L., Harald K., Holger B., Ilona H., Johanna K., Marcus W., Oliver M., Petra K., Rabea V., Sarah K., Thomas F., Ulf P., Uschi Z. - should I have forgotten someone he may forgive me for this.

Thank you!

8

About the author

We're just enthusiastic about what we do.

Steve Jobs

Frau Ordnung lives, laughs and writes in Stuttgart, Southern Germany.

Life as the oldest of four children has shaped her as much as founding her own family.

As a professional organizer and organizational coach, she helps people find more time and a ballast-free life with lean management in the household.

In her numerous courses and lectures, she gives insights into the work of an organization coach and valuable tips for the independent implementation of lean methods in the household.

She loves good books and prefers to spend her free time on a bike or in the great outdoors.

9

INDEX

5 Whys 45

5R's 58

5S 46, 110

7 forms of waste 40, 122

CIP 37, 116

Corona 23

Correction and defects 41

crafts 92

FIFO 50

First in First Out 50

garage 92

Garden 96

gym 92

HADOME 45

HANSEI 53, 108, 118

Hobbies 92

HomeOffice 88

Instagram 15

Inventory 41

Jidoka 60

KAIZEN 37, 116, 121

KANBAN 34, 112

KANBAN-Board 112

Kitchen 71

Literature 133

MUDA 40, 122

music 92

Overprocessing 44

Overproduction 40

Professional Organising 135

Pull-Principle 61

Reflection 56

SEIKETSU 51

SEIRI 48

SEISO 50

SEITON 49

Set in order 49

Shine 50

SHITSUKE 52

Sorting out 48

Standardize 51

Streams 113, 120

Success 118, 123

Twitter 15

Unnecessary movements
   44

Unnecessary Transport 43

Value of streams 113

Visualization 112

Waiting 42

NOTES

NOTES

NOTES

NOTES

NOTES